IF THESE WALLS COULD TALK

A HISTORY OF THE CHENOWETH FARM MANOR HOUSE

BETH THOMAS

Edited by
LYDIA SHERRER

IF THESE WALLS COULD TALK:

A History of the Chenoweth Farm Manor House

Copyright © 2020 by Beth Thomas

All rights reserved.

ISBN 13: 978-1-950267-97-2

Published by Chenoweth Press LLC 2020

Louisville, KY, USA

No part of this book may be reproduced in any form or by any electronic or mechanical means, including information storage and retrieval systems, without written permission from the author, except for the use of brief quotations in a book review.

This book is sold subject to the condition that it shall not, by way of trade or otherwise, be lent, resold, hired out, or otherwise circulated without the publisher's prior consent in any form of binding or cover other than that in which it is published and without a similar condition including this condition being imposed on the subsequent purchaser. Under no circumstances may any part of this book be photocopied for resale.

CONTENTS

Preface	v
1. Part 1: An Empire Needs an Empire House —1900 - 1919	1
2. Part 2: The Second Generation—1919 - 1985	25
3. Part 3: The Third and Fourth Generations—1985 - 2014	41
Appendix: The Thomas Generations r.e. Chenoweth Farm	69
About the Author	71

PREFACE

Have you ever wished you could be a fly on the wall? (Probably when your kids were at someone else's house!) Chenoweth House has had many flies! I know. I lived there for twenty-six years, and it is a farm, after all. And it had cows....But those kind of flies can't talk. What Chenoweth House *did* have is an attic full of letters and memorabilia. It was owned and lived in by members of the Thomas family from its construction in 1900 through 2014, when it was purchased by Paul and Pat Hornback and rechristened "Heritage House". What other home do you know of that has been continuously inhabited by the same family for over one hundred years and four generations?

When I married into the Thomas family in 1981, I quickly learned that the Thomas motto was, "Never throw anything away!" We moved to the Chenoweth Farm manor house, then affectionately known simply as "The Big House", in 1988 when my husband, Ted, came back to help run the family farm. Part of his employment agreement was to live in the big house and take care of it. So we moved from a 2-bedroom mobile home in Virginia, to this 8,000-plus square foot manor house in Kentucky. Ted's grandparents, having lived through the Depression, were avid adherers to the "never throw anything away" maxim. For awhile, this was the bane of my existence as I tried to carve out a living space in the house. Ted's grandparents were gone. Funny thing, though, they didn't take any of their possessions with them!

Front steps of Chenoweth House.

In the late 1990's, Emily Thomas (wife of BA III) hired a Louisville historian, one Paul Latimer, to research and write a history of Chenoweth Farm and the Thomas family. He found rich resources in the attic: family letters going all the way back to pre-Civil War years, original deeds from the 1800's, wills, and much more. Though never officially published, the Thomas family has a draft of Latimer's history in 3 spiral-bound volumes, as well as the original letters and documents he used for research. The task I have set for myself is to mine Mr. Latimer's extensive work for information about the house itself, and to add other anecdotes and pictures which have been passed down to me. I have relied heavily on Latimer's conclusions drawn from the original sources, without going back to those sources myself. This is not a good precedent for a historian, but I trust it will be sufficient for a storyteller. The research is Mr. Latimer's, the storytelling is mine. I hope you enjoy the result!

By the way, you might as well go ahead and flip to the appendix to familiarize yourself with the Thomas generations. Feel free to consult it frequently to avoid getting hopelessly lost with names in the following pages. You in the current living generations have probably heard many of these things before, but this is the first time they have ever been recorded in one place together. Absorb all the minute details, or flip through and read the stories. This is your heritage.

-Beth Thomas, January, 2020

1

PART 1: AN EMPIRE NEEDS AN EMPIRE HOUSE—1900 - 1919

Chenoweth House was built in the year 1900 by Wilson John (WJ) and Mary Thomas. WJ and his brother, Benjamin Allen, along with their ancestors, had spent the last 75 years acquiring land along Clear Creek in Shelby County. The Thomas ancestors were part of the Welsh Quaker migration to Pennsylvania, Morris and his wife arriving in 1768 with their 10 children. An eleventh child, Oswald, was born on American soil in 1769. He was WJ and BA's grandfather, who made his way via Hampshire Co., VA, to Harrodsburg, KY. Oswald Thomas purchased land along Fox Run in Shelby County in 1798. (Are you bored yet? Trust me, I'll get to the house very quickly! You won't *believe* how much I'm leaving out!)

It wasn't until 1825 that he made the first purchases of land along Clear Creek: the seeds of Chenoweth Farm. During his and the next two generations, much land was added by Oswald and various sons and grandsons, passed around amongst the family members, and eventually consolidated by Oswald's son Wilson, and his grandsons WJ and BA I. The last land purchase took place in 1913. The result was a small empire—3,320 acres under single ownership—the largest contiguous farm in the region (Latimer, p. 70)

Wilson Thomas, son of Oswald Thomas, father of Benjamin Allen (BA I) and Wilson John (WJ) Thomas

Nancy Johnston Thomas, wife of Wilson Thomas

WJ and Mary Thomas

BA Thomas I on the front porch of the manor house

Henrietta Stout Thomas, wife of BA Thomas I

Part 1: An Empire Needs an Empire House—1900 - 1919

An empire needed an empire house. In 1897, BA I's wife, Nettie, died. Mary took their son, Ben Allen (hereafter known as BA II), into her home to raise. She also had WJ's Aunt Paulina living with them until her death in 1889, was planning to bring her aging parents to live with them, and was beginning to feel cramped in their house. Mr Latimer relates, "It is said that Mary designed the house" (p.71). I don't know who said that, but it is a safe bet that the *impetus* for building the house came from Mary. The house was actually built by the firm of L.H. Gruber and Sons. I'll tell you more about them in just a moment. We have a copy of an ad by this firm that features a picture of Chenoweth House, which says, "designed and erected by L.H. Gruber and Sons". No doubt Mary participated in the design process, but the actual design was completed by the Gruber architects.

This firm consisted of Lewis H. Gruber and his sons, Lynn and Henry. Lynn was the architect, rated one of the best in Kentucky. The aforementioned ad lists a whole host of stores, banks, and residences which the Grubers built, including Harry Weissinger's "Undulata" (now home to well-known Saddlebred breeder Hoppy Bennett), and "Allen Dale" for Mrs. Bettie Meriwether, ancestor to the current Van Stockum owners. They also built the lovely chapel in Shelbyville's Grove Hill Cemetery, and the Shannon Funeral Home.

BA II was ten years old when the manor house was built. Among his many memories recorded on tape (and included in the Latimer history) are the following concerning the acquisition of the property and the building of the house:

> "When Uncle John married, he bought some land from Van Snook which is the site of the present Thomas home. The house they moved into was already there. It was later divided in two parts and moved to make way for the house Uncle John built. The land in

front of the yard south to Highway 43 was not included in this portion [which is where the entrance avenue is now] and his outlet to the road was through a very crooked and rough road that entered the Mulberry and Eminence Road, now Highway 43, near the Thornton Johnson place. A good portion of this old road is now under water from a lake that was built several years ago. They had no road prepared, it was just over the ground." (p. 56)

"When the new house was built in 1900, the old house was divided and part of it put on the east side next to the road and the other part on the west side. I had quite a time while building the house seeing things and walking around. I remember I took some big pieces of wood and put them on a pile of dirt that came from the cellar and used it as a sliding board. When part of the foundation was being laid, they had a cornerstone which is close to the cellar entrance outside. A mason jar with quite a few letters and other things were put in there as a memento to maybe be taken out someday." (p.101)

It is hard to tell the final resting place of the original house on the site. BA II seems to be saying that it was separated and incorporated into the new house, on the east and west sides, unless he means the east and west sides of the farm. Latimer describes it as having been moved to two separate places on the farm, and says that BA I lived in one of the halves. As you will see in a moment, it seems that both BA I and BA II lived with John and Mary in the new house, and Mary's parents did move in with them in 1902.

I have recently found what appears to be a dedicatory speech, or notes for such, presumably by WJ Thomas, dated July 25, 1900, on the occasion of the laying of the cornerstone of the house, and also when the "time capsule" would have been buried. It is not signed, sometimes being in a third person narrative form, but occasionally using first person pronouns. It reveals some of the family history, but also the Thomas' plans and hopes for their new home.

"This house was planned by Lynn Gruber, architect, Shelbyville, KY, after numerous interviews with Mr. and Mrs. W. J. Thomas (the owners), and in April of this good year 1900, dirt was broken; the building begun. Today we lay the cornerstone in the presence of many friends assembled to do honor to the occasion.

The Estate of WJ and BA Thomas consists of Eighteen Hundred acres in this one body and on this spot was the residence and farm of 200 acres formerly belonging to Van B. Snook (deceased) which was originally granted to Col. Allen for meritorious services during the war of the Revolution. The brothers were born one and one half miles southeast of this spot and have been partners all of our lives [note change of pronoun], keeping no individual accounts. Our Father Wilson Thomas died 1887—in his 82nd year. Our mother is still living in her ninety (94) fourth year—remarkably well-preserved for one so far advanced in age She was born in Loudon Co, VA Feb. 16th, 1807, was married November 8, 1832, celebrated her golden wedding in 1882. She has only 3 grandchildren: Wilson T. and Edward Crawford Layson, and Ben Allen Thomas, Jr., aged 10 years [BA II]. The last named is present and the prospective successor to this residence.

BA Thomas [I] is the Junior partner of the firm; father of Ben Allen Thomas, Jr., and was born June 2, 1842; was married to Nettie Stout of Woodford Co., Ky in Dec. 1, 1887. His wife died in Jan., 1896. WJ Thomas, the Senior partner was [born] Sept. 19, 1837; was married to Mary Henry Thomas in Nov 19, 1879.

After more than 20 years residence on this spot we this day join our friends in laying this cornerstone for our future residence, hoping that it may, as "a city that is set on a hill cannot be hid", always shed rays of happiness and good will in all directions among the human family. The family that will occupy this residence will be John Walker Thomas and his wife Elizabeth Giles [Mary's parents], who have passed the 3 score and ten limit of life and are spending their old days with their daughter; Mary Henry wife of WJ Thomas, BA Thomas [I] and his son Ben Allen Thomas Jr. make up the occupants of this home. The improvements are the latest and best known to the art of house building, and no pains or expense have been spared to make this house a lovely home in this, the last of the 19th century." [Which just goes to show that WJ, at least, believed that the 20th century started in 1901!]

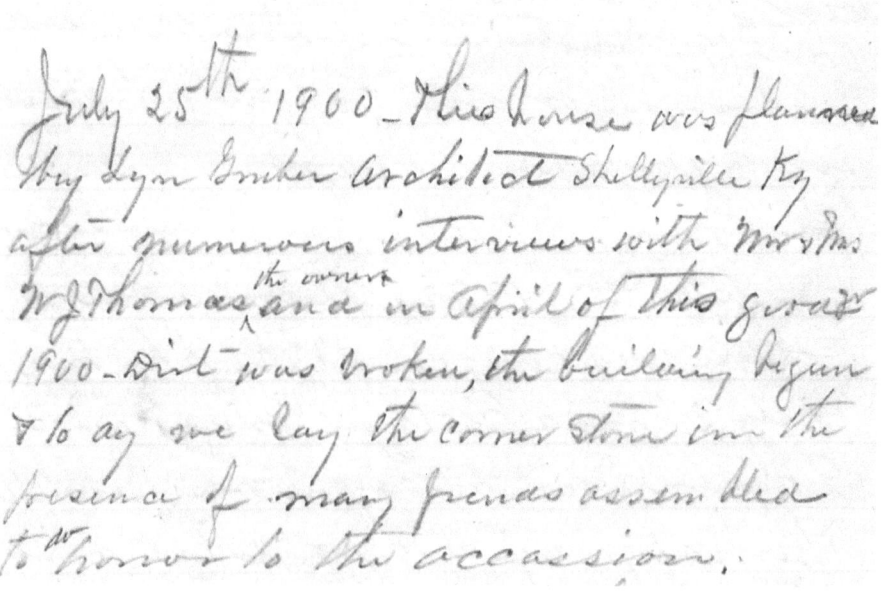

Excerpt of WJ's original hand-written dedication speech

REGARDING the expense that was not spared, Winford Thomas once told me that the house cost $40,000 to build in 1900. A quick Google search shows that $40,000 in 1900 is equivalent in purchasing power to $1,224,800 in the year 2020!

ARCHITECTURE

THIS SEEMS to be an appropriate place to give you some architectural details about the house. If that sort of thing doesn't interest you, feel free to skip to the next section and indulge in the stories and history. The following description is taken from the Kentucky Historic

Resource, Shelby County Nr. 55, and is in Latimer's appendix H, p. 302. Keep in mind that the grand main entrance faces the south. The compass points in the original are off by 45 degrees. I have corrected them in the following excerpt:

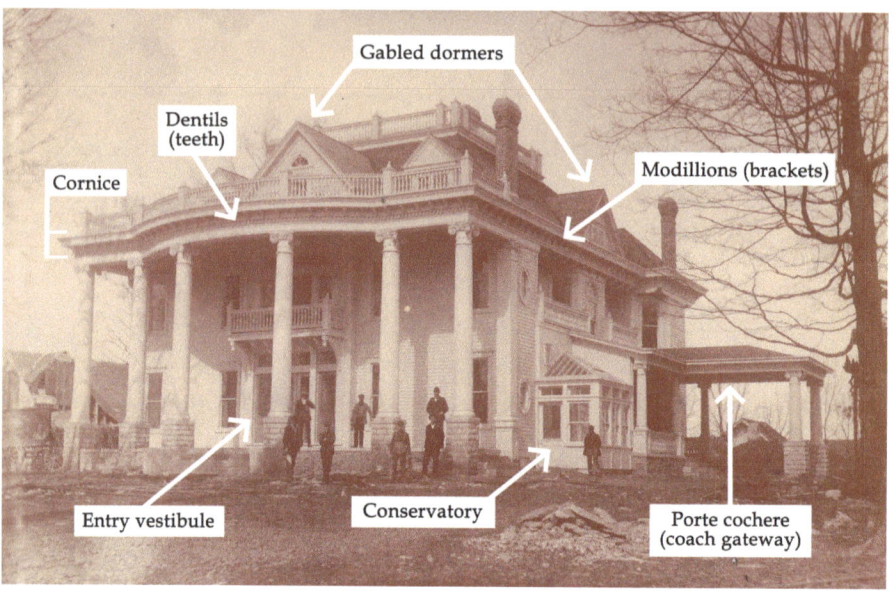

"The frame is sawn wood, the exterior is plain weatherboard and the foundation is rough-faced stone.

Exterior: The unusually large 2½ story 5-bay frame house incorporates elaborate Colonial Revival detailing, a flat-topped hipped roof with a gabled dormer on each of the three main fronts, as well as flanking pedimented dormers on the south front. The principal south front is completely sheltered by a colossal curve-fronted porch supported by fluted Ionic columns on stone plinths. The porch cornice, which is continuous with and identical to that on the entire house, is ornamented with dentils and modillions. The central entry bay projects slightly to form a vestibule, with sidelight and transoms, surmounted by a bracketted (sic) second floor balcony reached by a three-part opening spanned by an elliptical fanlight. The east front has inset and projecting bays, 2nd-floor balconies, and an Ionic porte cochere adjacent to a ground-level solarium or conservatory.

On the west a central one-story Ionic porch gives access to a stair hall, and is flanked on the north by a one-story bay. An ell to the north with an enclosed one-story porch gives onto the rear yard. The entire house has a complex floor plan that might be said to derive from the double-pile type, but is clearly of professional origin. From the south (sic) it appears to be a double-pile house with a two-room ell, while in plan and on the north (sic) it is clearly three rooms in depth, as if a conventional two-room ell was buried partially within a larger house.

Interior: A pair of parlors flank the center passage on the south. Dentillated cornices over interior openings. East parlor, reached by pocket door from passage, has mantel shelf supported on griffin-headed columns, leaf molding applied to ceiling. West parlor, also reached by pocket door from passage, has wood mantel on paired columns, wreaths and swags. Passage and west parlor ceilings have applied rope molding. Stair is located in passage to west off center passage, its landing lit by leaded glass window with elliptical fanlight. Rear rooms have bull's eye corner block trim on openings. Second set of stairs rises in narrower extension off center passage. Dining room on the west and two large rooms on the east each have polygonal projecting fronts."

There now, was that TMI (too much information)? I told you to skip it, remember. You should have listened! It is also worth noting that the original house, as far as I know, was equipped with acetylene lamps. The long tubes that come down from the ceiling, still seen today at least in the chandelier in the front hall (see below), were to conduct the acetylene. Every room and some of the halls had a fireplace for heat, being fitted up with Rumford fireplaces, designed for burning coal. These are shallower than a wood-burning fireplace. I have been told that there was one servant who did nothing else but tend the approximately seventeen fireplaces all day long.

It is interesting to note that even though means of communication have changed since 1900, other things have stayed the same regarding soliciting customers. Word of WJ's building project seems to have spread quickly despite the lack of modern technology. While going through a file box of WJ's from this first decade of the 1900's, I found numerous letters from companies associated with the construction industry, all of them trying to interest WJ in using their products. One of them was from a company advertising such lighting fixtures as the one described above. My favorite letter of the bunch, from the Aldine Manufacturing Company of Grand Rapids MI, maker of high grade wood mantels, "Jobbers of tile for facings, floors, vestibules, bathrooms, etc." begins this way: "May 28, 1900…Information of rather an indefinite nature has reached us that you are building or about to build a new residence in which you will, no doubt, require mantels, Grates, Tile, Etc.…"

Also not mentioned in the architectural description, but described to me by my husband, Ted, is the framing method used in the building. Chenoweth House was built using balloon framing, a technique popular when lots of long wood for studs was readily available. The framing studs run all the way from the bottom sill to the upper plate, and the upper floor framing is hung from these studs. This technique had the advantage over traditional post and beam framing with joinery, in that it took less-skilled labor, being nailed together. A disadvantage of this method is the conduit this makes for fire, with no fire stops in between the floors. There was also no insulation between the vertical studs. By the late 1940's, balloon framing was replaced by platform framing, also called "stick framing", where each floor is independently framed. (You can thank Google and Wikipedia for this fascinating information.)

. . .

The Legend of John Walker Thomas and the Dinner Bell

The only remaining thing to relate during this first period of ownership is a famous Thomas legend regarding Mary Thomas' brother, John Walker Thomas. (Mary's maiden name was also Thomas, though an unrelated family). John Walker had married a woman named Yeba, and had six children with her. He had a reputation as a crack shot, but also had chronic problems with alcoholism. He was often gone for long periods seeking his fortune, or drying out and going through rehab at one place or another. As a result, Yeba and the children were at times in desperate straits trying to make ends meet. She appealed to Mary in late 1908, not knowing what else to do. During that year, WJ and Mary brought the older four of the children to live at their home. Yeba took the younger two children and sought refuge with her sister and brother-in-law in Ft. Thomas, KY. She had sued for divorce and custody of the children. (The last picture we have of Yeba and all her children shows seven, and seven are listed in the 1910 census. The youngest, also Yeba, was born in 1909, so we can assume Yeba, the mother, was pregnant at this time).

While John was "seeking a cure" at Hot Springs, Arkansas—a trip arranged and paid for by WJ—WJ foreclosed and sold the farm property where John and his family had been living, in order to pay John's debts. Mary wrote to her brother to inform him that it had been sold, and to offer the proposal that John and his family could live with them. Yeba and the children would live with them with or without John, she said. John adamantly rejected this idea, pawned his watch and pin, and high-tailed it back to Shelby County. He moved back into the sold-yet-still-vacant house, planning to reclaim his wife and children, and making threats to WJ and family.

WJ moved his family into Shelbyville, leaving a guard at the big house. Mulberry school was closed because the teacher roomed with the Thomases, and he also removed into town. (The central bedroom on the west side with the knocker on the door is the room where the teachers stayed. This practice had already started in the early 1900's.)

Yeba and her children around 1910: Elizabeth (1897), Mary (1900), Ruth (1901), Francis (1902), Sarah (1904), John Walker (1907), Yeba (1909)

The details of the next week need not be told, but it was daily reported in the Louisville paper, and was a sensation at the time. John barricaded himself in his old house for awhile. Prior to this, however, he had made a trip into town to complain to Judge Davis about his children being taken from him. Because there was a warrant for his arrest, someone called the police. The police went straight out to WJ's house, not finding John because he went to Shelbyville first. But John then left for the house before the police could get back. He passed them on his way to WJ's house, persuading them by strength of arms to keep going to Shelbyville and leave him alone!

The guard fled at his approach, so John entered the manor house unopposed. Here are his own words of what happened next:

> "As I entered the house the 'phone was ringing. I took down the receiver to answer the call, which was from WJ at Shelbyville. He talked as though he was excited very greatly, and he said: 'That fellow'—I suppose meaning me—'is on his way out there. He flashed a gun on the Sheriff and you had better look out.' Having delivered himself of this awful message, I thought it best to tell him as calmly as I could [note: WJ claimed that John greeted him with a string of curses.] who was at the phone. He must have had a fit when I told him.
>
> The statement that I did some shooting while on the premises of WJ on that visit is true, but the damage done was to the top of an old pump that would bring about one dollar. My only reason for shooting was to show that I was there." (p.78)

John doesn't mention in this statement, but it was reported in the paper that he also shot the dinner bell, and this is what intersects with our subject of Chenoweth House. This bell ended up at some point on the ground beside the root cellar. Over the years it sank into the ground and was covered with leaves. The roots of a maple tree grew around it. In 2012, my daughters excavated around it enough to prove that it was a bell, and to take a picture of the bullet hole and percussion ring visible from John Walker's shot. We hope that one day the Hornbacks (who purchased the house and property in 2014) will be able to unearth it and hang it up again, to be visual evidence for this story.

Partially buried dinner bell with bullet hole over halfway down the side

John eventually turned himself in, and agreed to go to California, never to return, for a monthly stipend of $30 from WJ. WJ also agreed to pay all court costs, and assume the care of Yeba and the children. John left on March 13, 1909. It was not to be a "happily ever after" ending, however. John settled in Salinas, CA, and the family received occasional post cards for the next three years. In 1912, they received a letter from a sheriff reporting that John was very ill, then a post card reporting his death. He was later shipped home in a coffin. Mr. Shannon, the undertaker (whose grandson is still in business in Shelbyville), called WJ to come view the body. When he did, he found that there was a bullet hole through the chest. WJ hired a detective to investigate, but the mystery of John's death was never solved. Mr. Latimer does not give a source for this information. The newspaper obituary from the Salinas Valley *Rustler* (September 19, 1912) just says that John had been suffering from Bright's disease (nephritis, a kidney disease), was found in his hotel room, and lists the cause of death as acute alcoholism.

THOMAS HOUSEHOLD in 1910

Chenoweth House, early 1900s: WJ (standing), Mary (bench right), Yeba (bench left), one of Yeba's daughters at her feet (possibly Francis or Sarah), plus unknown child (far left)

We can see a glimpse, then, of the Thomas household about this time by looking at the 1910 census. Besides listing WJ and Mary, it includes both BA I and BA II as living in the household, along with four nieces: Elizabeth, Mary, Ruth, and Francis. These would be Yeba's daughters. We're not sure if Yeba and her other three children ever joined the household. Additional household members were Mary's father; H.G. Wells, the overseer; and Mary White, the boarding schoolteacher, probably for Mulberry School. In his recorded memories, BA II mentions Mr. Hinton Wells, who came to live with them in 1902. Ben Allen was twelve, and Mr. Wells was twenty-two. He became like a big brother to the young Thomas boy, and stayed with them until 1910, in which year he married and went to live elsewhere on the farm.

H.G. Wells (left) and BA II (right) circa 1910

In 1904, WJ took BA II and Hinton Wells to the Louisiana Purchase Exposition, held in St Louis to commemorate the centennial. I mention this here because of the two large frames of birds under glass that hung in the breakfast room during our residence—one containing mallards, and one of ruffed grouse (see below).

Winford once told me that Granddaddy Thomas (BA II) brought these home from the 1927 St. Louis Exposition. An internet search, however, reveals no World's Fair anywhere in the US in this year, and there is no mention of any such trip in 1927 in the Thomas history. We can then assume they were bought on this 1904 trip, which is described in detail by BA II in his recollections. (So much for the accuracy of "I was told"....)

It is also curious to me that there is so little mention of BA I in Latimer's history. While WJ was more of a businessman involved in banking, BA I was the one involved in farming. What letters we have between BA father and son are affectionate. In one, BA I relates a sermon he had just heard about the prodigal son, and goes on to counsel his son about the ill effects of using tobacco. Benjamin Allen Thomas died in 1912 shortly after John Walker Thomas, when BA II was twenty-two, and so disappears from our story. BA II, along with Hinton Wells, assumed the responsibility for running the farm.

2

PART 2: THE SECOND GENERATION —1919 - 1985

Ben Allen II and Vestina Bailey Thomas

In January of 1919, BA II brought home a new mistress for the big house. He had waited until after his Aunt Mary died (1918) to marry, because he did not think the house should have two mistresses in residence at the same time. He would have been twenty-seven years old. BA II was the only descendant of either of Wilson Thomas' sons, and would become the recipient of the house and farm estate, and the one to carry on its heritage. I am assuming that Uncle John (WJ Thomas) was still residing in the house, until his death in 1925. The 1920 census lists the household as containing WJ, BA II, Vestina, and boarder Philomon Bird. Yeba's family was by then no longer part of the household.

BA II and Vestina added two sons to the family in the house: BA III in 1920 (obviously after the census), and Winford in 1924. The family cradle, still in the house today, would have been in use for these occasions. Ben Allen grew up in the southeast second floor bedroom, for his desk and some of his childhood belongings were still there when we arrived in 1988!

Thomas family cradle holding Lydia Thomas, granddaughter to BA III, June 1989

The 1930 census, minus WJ, adds BA III and Winford, three boarders: Bess Wright, Estelle McConnel, and Fannie McBurney; and four servants: Tom, Minnie, Margaret, and Mildred Washington. Latimer states that Tom and Minnie lived in the servant's cabin north of the root cellar, and were the last to occupy that structure (p. 303). I think that Miss Wright was the school teacher, but am not sure. She became a dear friend of the Thomas family—someone whom I met in later years. She gave us a quilted pillow when we married, which stayed in our bedroom chair for thirty years until it finally wore out.

Winford Thomas (left) and BA III (right) with Bess Wright, circa 1927

Vestina and BA II with little BA III on the front steps of Chenoweth House, 1920

Part 2: The Second Generation—1919 - 1985

Winford Thomas (left) and BA III (right) as teens

Changes to the House and Grounds

Although the basic structure of the house did not change during this period (1919 - 1985), there were inevitable changes as new technology was developed, and as Vestina exercised her love of flowers on the surrounding grounds. An exception would be the removal of the railings around the upper flat roof and the roof on top of the front porch. I cannot date this removal. Ted remembers his dad (BA III) saying that they were removed relatively soon after the house was built. There was a problem with leakage where the posts attached to the roof. A picture of the house dated 1935 – 1940 shows the upper railings gone, but the ones above the front porch still in place. The next picture from the 1960's shows all the railings removed.

Manor house circa 1935-1940 with porch railing still intact

Electricity: Probably the first major change would have been the conversion from acetylene to electric lighting. Most folks in major cities and towns had electricity by the 1930's, but it may have been after 1936 and the passage of the Rural Electrification Act that electricity made it out to Chenoweth Farm. Most of BA II's recorded memories deal more with farming practices, and don't mention these changes to the house. However, his associate, Ryburn Weakley, stated that electric lines were run out his road in 1937 by the Rural Electric Cooperative that had been formed. (Latimer, p.118) We can assume that they came to Chenoweth Farm about the same time.

Manor house in the 1960s with porch railing removed.

Heating: Another change that must have been welcomed was the installation of a coal-fired furnace in the cellar, and a system of radiators and pipes to heat the entire house. Even though most of the pipes didn't run inside the walls, what a disruption and tearing-up-of-plaster that must have entailed! I can't believe we haven't found any written descriptions. What used to occupy a servant for all hours of the day could now be done by one person once every few hours. Ted remembers Granddaddy Thomas (BA II) describing how he used to have to wake up every two hours during the night to stoke the furnace. A large hopper with an auger was later installed, so that one could fill up the hopper, and the auger would gradually feed the coal into the furnace through the night (or day). Presumably, in the process of installing the radiators, some of the fireplaces were removed, such as one that was in the slanted wall at the north end of the front hall. At present, there remain twelve fireplaces.

Plumbing: Somewhere along the way, indoor plumbing would have been installed as well. The change would have been made from hot and cold running servants to hot and cold running water. At some point after running water was put in, a fire hose was installed in the upstairs back hall closet. Firefighters spend lots of time tending to their hoses so they remain in operable condition. I was told that BA II actually had one occasion to use the fire hose. When he turned it on, the water sprayed out of the sides at many different points due to dry rot. What a disappointment!

Security: BA II employed many day workers on the farm, and needed cash to pay them. Sometime during the history of the house, a safe was installed in the upstairs farm office to hold the cash to pay the workers. It is still there to this day. This is entirely due to the fact that it is a BIG Mama "Hall's Patent" safe which I have been told weighs half a ton, literally. There is some disagreement between those of us who "have been told" but our recollections range from 1,000 to 1,700 pounds. In any case, it is extremely heavy! It reached the office via the dumbwaiter that used to be in what is now a central closet on the first and second floors. You can still see the mechanism for it in the attic, but the shaft has been divided into closets on each floor. There is now no way to remove the safe that will bear the weight! Someone may prove me wrong one day, but this is what I have been told.

The dumbwaiter mechanism located in the house attic

One of my favorite stories about the house relates to the above dumbwaiter. Vestina once asked one of the male servants to bring down a sack of flour from the attic. He asked, "What do I use to bring it down?" Vestina said, "Use the dumbwaiter!" A few minutes later, he returned asking for an old sheet, which Vestina produced. Said servant proceeded to the attic where he carefully spread the old sheet on the floor of the dumbwaiter, *opened* the sack of flour, and poured it into the dumbwaiter! If you have any experience at all with pouring flour, you can visualize what happened next: the flour went "woosh" down the shaft and out into the downstairs for quite a distance. It took days to clean up, and you can believe that even though I don't know his name, that servant's name was "mud" for many days with Vestina. BA III later told me that the servant was Tom Washington, and that they were finding flour in the drawers for more than a year!

Fitness: Another thing BA II was known for was his commitment to physical fitness, so much so that he installed fitness equipment in the house. There are two attachment points on the ceiling of the back hall downstairs where he had hung a set of exercise rings. The first time BA III brought his future wife, Emily, to the house, she ran into the rings and banged her head as she rounded the corner! Emily described this incident to me, and spoke of being stunned for long moments, and embarrassed in front of her future in-laws. BA II also installed a chin-up bar in the doorway of the upstairs southeast bedroom, and kept a wrestling mat, punching bag, and barbells in the attic. There are many stories of BA II gathering the workers around in a barn during bad weather, and challenging them to wrestle, one after the other, saving the strongest for last. But I digress. I'm supposed to be talking about the house!

At some point, a clay tennis court was added southwest of the house, across the yard fence in the garden area. It is now grass-grown, but there are pictures of BA II and his cousins playing on the court.

Gardens: Vestina gained a national reputation as a bulb grower, with hemerocallis (day lilies), gladioli, and notably with daffodils. She was very involved in the Shelby County Homemakers, and promoted the planting of thousands of daffodils around Shelby County. If you see daffodils naturalized along roadsides around the county, it is probably due to her influence. There are now hundreds of daffodils naturalized on the Chenoweth property from those Vestina and her helpers planted years ago. She had a main garden to the west of the house, with grass paths, where there were 250 labeled varieties of daffodils. In the spring, members of the Homemakers would come out to view the blossoms, and then place orders for their favorites. Vestina would aggregate the orders, and place one huge order with her preferred Dutch bulb grower. When the bulbs arrived, she would then divide them all up into the individual orders to distribute to the members.

Vestina described her impetus to share the joy of four new daffodil varieties whose bulbs had been sent to her by her brother-in-law, Ben Logan. When they bloomed in the spring of 1938, they cheered and encouraged her so much amidst the gloomy financial times, that she wanted to share them with other farm wives.

> "If a few daffodil bulbs could give me so much pleasure and help me to forget my troubles, surely I could find some way to pass this enjoyment along to other farm women who must be in the same position we were. Hurried telephone calls to all the Landscape Leaders of the Shelby County Homemakers brought them to my home on a stated day to see my daffodils. As April weather is always unpredictable, I gathered a single stem of each variety, labelled it, put it in a soft drink bottle, and placed it with all of my old varieties on a card table for display. The afternoon was well spent for each guest went home with the desire to grow some like them. That fall I ordered a few more varieties for myself, and when daffodil time came again, I invited the Landscape Leaders to meet with me again, this time for the day, for they were to bring whatever varieties they grew, and we would display all of them. And so the Shelby County Homemakers Daffodil Show was born...." (written account by Vestina, not dated, possibly a speech given to a garden club).

Vestina continued to host the annual Daffodil Show for sixteen years, (entertaining the judges at luncheon while the exhibitors classified their entries on the back porch to then display in the front rooms of the house) until it outgrew the house and had to be held in a public venue. The show was open to the public on Saturday, and Sunday afternoon. "Frequently during those two days our registration book would show that we had had over 1,000 guests: looking at the Daffodil Show in the house; at my display in the sunroom (I did not compete); or wandering over the grounds jotting down the names of the varieties they wanted to order the next fall."

According to her account, she started the bulb cooperative in the fall of 1939, by taking it upon herself to order a small stock of bulbs for each "club" at her own expense, then selling them to the clubs to sell to members. She did this with trepidation, since no one really had spending money, least of all for flowers! From that small beginning, her orders expanded to include clubs from all over Kentucky, and once, all the state parks in Kentucky! In addition to daffodils, there were orders for tulips, hyacinths, scilla, crocus, lilies, glads, and later daylilies. She ordered from companies all over the world, always fronting the money, sorting and dividing all the bulbs herself into labeled sacks for each lady, and receiving payment when the clubs received their orders. She stated, "Since 1939 I have purchased over 100,000 daffodil bulbs alone, and the other bulbs, all added together would be over twice that number. This has been at a cost well over $35,000."

Ribbon awarded to Vestina circa 1965 for her many years of exceptional daffodils

Vestina (far left) circa 1965 at a Daffodil Show

One day, I will again find the letter we have from a Dutch bulb grower's representative, who wrote to Vestina requesting to meet her when he was in the area. He wanted to see for himself the person who placed such enormous orders! I have been told that she also did bulb trials for some of the growers, to test the bulbs' performance in this area. Although the bulb drying shed has long since fallen down, you can still see the daffodils growing in test rows further to the west, before the large pasture. There is also an area south of the main daffodil garden where English Wood Hyacinths appear in May, after the April daffodil show.

Daffodil test rows and collapsed bulb-drying shed, 1989

Vestina in her vast daffodil garden west of the house, 1975. In its prime it held over 250 labeled varieties

The House Ages

BA II was known as a go-getter for most of the years of his life. He was an astute businessman, and not afraid to take risks when needed. He was an advocate of saving, and helped many of the farm partners to acquire their own farms. One can imagine that during his prime, and while Vestina had a corp of servants to help in the house and grounds, that it remained a showplace. Just think of the magnitude of the modernizations that he superintended during his lifetime, as outlined above! He lived in the house for eighty-five years–almost unheard of in this day and age.

Inevitably, though, both Ben Allen and Vestina aged and became less able to keep the house in shape. You might say that they and the house grew old together. In her later years, Vestina became rather paranoid, and did not want strangers in the house. That precluded having any workmen around for remodeling.

Emily Thomas relates that after Vestina died in 1984, she and Winford's daughter, Bebe Thomas, persuaded BA II to begin remodeling some of the rooms. They got as far as completing the southeast bedroom and adjoining sitting room before his death in 1985. And that, as they say, ends a tale. Chenoweth House would have to wait many years for further renovations.

3

PART 3: THE THIRD AND FOURTH GENERATIONS—1985 - 2014

Ben Allen and Winford Thomas
Ted and Beth Thomas Family

This section is going to be an "as I recall it" section, since I participated in most of it. I have lumped these two generations together, as far as the house is concerned. Neither BA III nor Winford lived in the house as adults, but they had ownership and control of it. The farm office was in the house, so they were there every day, anyway. Ted and I lived there, beginning in 1988, but had neither ownership nor control. As you can imagine, this made for some awkward situations.

Both Winford's and BA III's wives had successfully campaigned for a home of their own. Winford built his wife, Betty, a lovely home on Colony Drive in Shelbyville. BA chose a plot on the east side of the farm, fronting Route 43, for his brick rancher. I would say that in both cases, following in Mary's tradition, the wives were the driving force, and participated in the design process. The BA III home was built in the early sixties, and Winford's prior to that.

Winford's wife, Betty, had already died of cancer (1970) before BA II died in 1985. After his father's death, Winford spent a lot of his time at the big house so it would not sit empty.

Brothers and partners BAT III (left) and Winford (right), 2005

When we moved to the big house in 1988, Winford would go back to Colony drive to sleep, but was at the farmhouse most of the rest of the time. He kept a stash of canned goods there, warmed his meals there, and took his Saturday night bath there. We described the arrangement as having an "installed Uncle".

As I have stated before, neither BA II nor Vestina took any of their things with them when they died. In 1988, when we arrived, there the things were still, along with stacks of mail and papers and farm tools that had accumulated since their deaths. We had to stay with Ted's parents for several weeks while I carved out a living space for us that was safe for Sarah and Andrew, then ages four and one. Andrew spent these weeks incarcerated in a large, expandable wooden play area that we put in the parlor, which had remained miraculously free of farm clutter over the years. My theory? This room had been for guests when the Thomas boys were growing up, so it was *off limits* in their minds, and thus remained clear. Our family was granted the east side of the upstairs for our living area. This worked out very well, since all four rooms were interconnected. We could shut the doors to the halls, and be very private going back and forth between our own rooms. Before we could move into any rooms, however, I had to pack away BA II and Vestina's things from all the drawers, closets, and kitchen cabinets. The Thomas motto was still in effect: Never throw anything away! Into boxes it all went, and up to the attic. The Hornbacks are probably still going through some of it! Just for the record, I have the distinction of being the first mistress of the house to function without servants. So I had four children and trained them to work!

Edward (Ted) Thomas family 1998 (left to right): Sarah (1984), Lydia (1989), Ted (1953), Serena (1992), Beth (1955), Andrew (1987)

Chenoweth House front (south facing) 1988. My mother reminded me after we moved that as a girl, I always said I wanted to live in a white farm house in the country. I never imagined it would look like this!

Part 3: The Third and Fourth Generations—1985 - 2014

Chenoweth House rear (north facing) 1988

Small northwest porch with pump and two peafowl 1988. The buried dinner bell with the bullet hole in it is located approximately ten feet to the right of the picture's edge, on the north side of the entrance to the root cellar

Room Use in this Era

During our tenure at the house, the farm office remained in use as such, and the downstairs middle east room with the graceful curved-top, built-in shelves served as the mens' (Winford and BA III) sitting room during the day. Here, they read the papers, watched TV, and had a good view of the east porch where farm workers would come to consult with them. My children have happy memories of sitting on one or the other of the men's laps and being read the funnies, or watching "Andy Griffith" with Uncle Winford. The large room across the hall to the north became our family room. This had earlier been a bedroom/sitting room during Vestina's failing years, since it has a small dressing room and bathroom attached.

Music room in the 1950s; looked much the same in 1988

The large parlor on the southwest corner remained a parlor and music room, bringing many happy hours of enjoyment to our children once they learned to play the piano. The Steinway baby grand that BA II purchased for Vestina remains and saw frequent use from the nineties until we left in 2014. The smaller parlor on the southeast side, with the griffin mantelpiece, eventually became Ted's office. It was filled with a wood and metal frame which held servers and computer paraphernalia, and was attached to only door and window frames to avoid any damage to the walls.

The small parlor in the 1950s; looked much the same in 1988

Our family ate meals in the breakfast room. The large dining room was a storage room for the first eighteen years we were there. We did finally clear it out in 2005 so that it once again was the site of many entertainments. I particularly loved what I called the "stretch dining table". With no leaves inserted, this table collapses to a 5 X 5 foot square. We used it this way only once, to prove that it would collapse all the way. But there are ten leaves, each twelve inches wide, making a fifteen-foot table with all the leaves inserted. The most leaves I ever remember using was six, for an eleven-foot table that would seat fourteen. I ordered two tablecloths to be used together to cover this length of table. The Thomas motto bore fruit when I was refurbishing the dining room after we cleared it out. Upstairs in the linen closet, I remembered seeing a box of sheer curtain panels. When I looked, there were three unopened packages, just the right size for those windows! In the drawers of the large buffet, I found three pairs of lovely flower medallions that screwed into the window frames to hold back the curtains.

Stretch dining table set for a ladies' tea party seating twelve, 2011

When we arrived, the alcove in the kitchen housed a cast iron cookstove. Vestina had kept it there to use in case the electricity went out. We had it moved out to the garage in order to put a washer and dryer in that space. Another item in the kitchen that fascinated the children was the crank phone on the wall behind the pass-through door. This phone used to connect to the farm shop (another "I was told" item). In the back entry, outside the kitchen, there was a large electric icebox when we arrived. We used this workhorse for many years for extra refrigeration space, until it finally faltered around 2012.

Upstairs, we eventually were able to expand into both the south and north bedrooms on the west side, as we added two more children and they grew older. That bedroom in the north ell was particularly pleasant since it has windows on three sides. We never used the center bedroom on the west side. That was Winford's room, and sacrosanct! He used to keep snickers bars in there hidden in a drawer. It was a big treat when he brought one out and cut it in pieces to parcel out to his great nieces and nephew. Since we home schooled our children, we also used the upstairs front hall as our schoolroom, it being about fourteen feet wide.

As you can imagine, our children loved to open the doors to our bedrooms and chase each other around and around in a big circle from the bedrooms, through the hall, and into the bedrooms again on the other end of the house. This was also a fantastic house in which to play hide and seek and "sardines" (sort of a reverse version of hide and seek where the seekers join the hider in his hiding place and get squished in like sardines until everybody has found the hiding place). Either of these games was most fun in the dark!

Architectural Crisis Intervention

As an outsider coming in, I could see the cracked plaster and peeling wallpaper, and wonder why there were no plans for renovation. The men, on the other hand, being raised during the depression, were extremely thrifty and conservative with regard to spending money. I remember Winford bragging once about what good shape the wallpaper in the front hall was in. Well, it was...compared to the rest of the house...and considering its age....I guess they had the "if it ain't broke, don't fix it" mentality. Also "if it *is* broke, find or manufacture the parts and fix it yourself." This accounted for the broken things saved in the attic, and the mounds of rusting machinery scattered about the farm. They might be needed for parts, you know. Though their thrift resulted in the accumulation of junky stuff, it also resulted in the perpetuation of Chenoweth Farm, even during harder times, and no accumulation of debt—an admirable feat.

Front porch roof in need of repair, October 1989

Porch and Roof Repair: Ted was, by default, the maintenance foreman on the farm, and also responsible for maintaining the house.

Any capital expenditures were to be covered by the owners, so any maintenance of that sort required the approval of BA III and Winford. By 1989, it became apparent to Ted that the front porch roof needed attention. After much research and persuasion of the men, he hired Sam Zena of Artisan Builders & Remodelers, Inc., out of Louisville to do the job in the fall of that year. Zena's company specialized in renovating historic homes. Before any work began, the honeybees in the end columns had to be dealt with. When Zena and his crew began tearing out rotten parts and assessing the repair needed, it was more extensive than originally thought. He ended up having to rebuild a major part of the curved front of the porch roof. I remember when the semi truck arrived bearing all the scaffolding, and maneuvered into the yard. The children were fascinated. It was hard to keep four-year-old Andrew away from the construction.

Here are Ted's words from my album that year: "Because there was extensive damage to the rotunda, the contractor built a box beam that was 3 feet by 25 feet by 6 inches thick inside the box truss which holds up the porch roof." Much of the ornate molding on the cornice had to be replaced, as well as some of the tongue-in-groove planking on the porch ceiling. Also repaired were the roofs of the porch and bay on the west side.

Chenoweth House after porch roof repair, late fall 1989

Another roofline repair that approached crisis proportions was the state of the chimneys, which were dropping bricks in bad storms and damaging the roof. Winford rejected what he thought were exorbitant estimates, and finally agreed to the cheapest alternative he could find, which involved taking down the highest layers of bricks (the curving section), and repairing what was left. Compare the height and shape of the chimneys in the following pictures, from 1946 and 2014. Unfortunately, this stop-gap measure did not solve the problem for very long.

In 1995, Ted replaced the roof over the back porch with a seamed metal roof. By the late 1990's, the roof on the rest of the house was in need of replacement. It wasn't until 2005, though, that Ted was able to get agreement to have this done. With a roof of this size, everything couldn't be done all in a day. There was one point when the front part of the house was covered with only roofing paper that we had a downpour early in the morning. There was a place in a dormer "valley" over our bedroom where (we discovered afterward) a workman's boot had punched a hole in the paper. I awoke to the sound of heavy dripping in a corner of the bedroom, right over the antique roll-top desk. I sprang out of bed and into action, grabbing towels from the nearby bathroom. Since the leaking water was the color of tea, I tore off my nightgown so it wouldn't be stained, and dashed around naked finding dishpans, laundry baskets, anything to catch the flow! Thankfully, no one else was upstairs at the front, and we did not yet have security cameras around the house! The next summer, we hired Sarah and Lydia to clean the roofing grit out of the attic. In the process we took the opportunity to get rid of trash, dirty old mattresses with their rusted springs, and broken items (including BA II's old wrestling mat that was so big, heavy, and dirty that it had to be thrown from the front porch roof to get it to the ground).

Home Education

THERE WAS one other advantage of a historic home with decades of accumulated contents: No matter what time period we were studying, there always seemed to be something in the house that related. For Ancient Greece, there were the ionic columns supporting the front porch, and various bronze statues and krater-shaped bowls that we used during a Greek feast. The book of Frederic Remington plates informed our study of him and the American West, and there was also a book of James Audubon's bird plates. Norman Rockwell's art?

Check. Studying Arabia? Didn't I see an English translation of the Koran, and Kahlil Gibran's *The Prophet*? There were the old clothes for dress-up, and for dramatizing historical periods; Great Uncle John's Civil War era saber, and other treasures in the attic. Add to that all the space for outdoor exploration, nature study, and hosting co-op days, and you ended up with an exceptional educational environment.

Moroccan souk dramatization done by our home school co-op group in the downstairs front hall in 1998. We covered the floor with brown paper to mimic the bare ground of the market and the older children manned "booths" while the younger children went shopping for various assigned items.

Climate Control

None of the improvements to the house during the 1900's included air-conditioning. The method of dealing with overheating was as follows: At night, when it was cool, one opened the windows, as well as the attic door. When it had been particularly hot during the day, one of us would also go up and open the hatch door at the very top of the roof (when no rain was forecast). This would allow the heat to be drawn out of the house just like smoke out of a chimney. The next day, as the outside temperature heated up to equal the inside, one would close the windows and draw the shades. With the eleven-foot ceilings, this kept the inside temperatures bearable unless there was an extended period of temperature in the 90's when it hardly cooled off at night. It did not, however, ameliorate the humidity. We installed ceiling fans in the rooms we used the most, which helped a lot. When the roof was replaced, we also installed two exhaust fans in the attic.

Heating was another story. With largely uninsulated walls, and a drafty house, heating was expensive, even using coal. The radiant heat from the radiators was lovely; much nicer than air blowing out of a vent. But it did not cancel out the cold floors and drafts from around the windows. Every June, the coal man from Eastern Kentucky would visit to see how much coal we wanted to purchase for the winter. The Thomas men would buy it in the summer when the price was the lowest. A few weeks later, he would come again in a large dump truck filled with coal. There were two rooms in the basement for the coal, one on each side of the house, which he would fill over two days. This was done using an auger in a chute that went from the back of the truck down through a window into the cellar. The coal transfer was always a spectator sport for my children.

Ted Thomas in his coal protection suit, winter 1991

Keeping the furnace going in the winter wasn't too bad using the large hopper to feed the furnace. You could usually fill it in the morning, and again at night before bed. There was one winter, however, that stands out in our memory. The coal was usually coated with some kind of oil, to cut down the coal dust. One year, however, either this was not done, or we received a cheaper grade that lacked the coating. Whomever went down to fill the hopper had to wear a respiratory mask, and clean their feet well when they came back up! I did lots of cleaning that winter. Even in the best of times, surfaces in the house, especially windows, would get coated with a thin film of blackness. I had several decorations that I never unwrapped and put out as long as we lived in that house, to protect them from the coal residue coating. The biggest aggravation occurred when the furnace went out for some reason, but the hopper was loaded with coal. The auger would keep feeding coal into the furnace. Ted would have to shovel it all out again in order to relight the furnace.

Finally, around 2008, Ted could no longer find parts to repair the coal furnace. It had to be replaced by a propane furnace. I rejoiced! No more coal or coal residue! Of course, I was not the one who would be paying the propane bill, which was quite a bit more than coal.

• • •

Entertaining

Such a large, elegant home just begged to be shared with others. You could say that Mary Thomas started it all when, in 1917, she used her thirty-eighth wedding anniversary as an excuse for a reunion of eighty-two of the wives and daughters of the men who contributed to the development of what she called Chenoweth Spring Farm. (Latimer, p. 86) Of course, Vestina hosted many flower shows there, and always had a big meal in the middle of the day for "the men". Ted has many fond memories of his grandmother pressing second helpings of cake on him! During our residence, the house was the setting for large Christmas gatherings, formal teas, lock-ins for the Chamber Choir of the Louisville Youth Choir, large church picnics, overnights for traveling Wycliffe missionaries home on furlough, and many a family gathering.

1990 gathering of friends and family including Graham cousins, Lucy Falconer's family (England) and Stephen Thomas' family (California)

On our first or second Christmas, Ted's mother (Emily) and I cooperated on a large open house. The agreement was that I would provide the place (cleaned and decorated), and she would provide the food. She brought me *all* her boxes of Christmas decorations, and said she did *not* want them back!

One large and memorable entertainment was pulled off by Emily, who wanted to mark the house's centennial in the year 2000. She invited everyone she could locate who had lived or worked on Chenoweth Farm, or the descendants thereof, to a Homecoming. She had a long list that she sent written invitations to, and she also had an article placed in the local paper for anyone she might have missed. The "party" was in the front yard, with a catered barbecued meal. We opened the downstairs of the house for tours, and I spent the afternoon taking eight groups of twenty-five through the house and telling stories.

Ben Allen III speaking at the beginning of a tour, July 2000 Homecoming Picnic

I don't have a record of total attendance, but about 200 folks went through the house. Paul Latimer was there interviewing anyone who had a story to tell about the farm, and some of these accounts appear in his history.

Partner Banquet, 2005. Andrew Thomas (left) and friend Caleb Harris (right) acted as butlers and servers for the evening. Emily Thomas (aka Nana, middle) was so proud of Andrew and called him her "TD&H" grandson: tall, dark, and handsome.

After we cleared out the dining room in 2005, we had the dining space to host a Partner Banquet. This was an occasion to honor past and present farm partners as Chenoweth Farm moved out of tobacco, dairy, and beef (farmed by partners in shares), and into leased crop arrangements. The dining room was also the scene of multiple afternoon teas, usually put on by our youngest daughter, Serena, for Emily (Nana) and her friends and bridge club members. We used the lovely Haviland Limoges china that belonged to Vestina, but also other single place settings that we had collected for the teas. I think Emily became hooked on teas through the influence of her daughter Lucy, who married an Englishman, and lived in England. She passed down the tradition to all three of my girls, who never miss a chance to go to tea!

Tea in the springtime was especially fine because we could pick dozens and dozens of daffodils from Vestina's garden to decorate the tables. Whichever child was assigned to gather the flowers would use one of Vestina's original cutting buckets

Passing the Baton

Chenoweth House had been included in a section of the farm set aside in a trust by BAT II, for the livelihood of his sons, and to be passed to his six grandchildren (four from BA III, and two from Winford). After Winford died in 2011, and BA III was experiencing declining mental functioning from Alzheimer's, the decision-making about the house devolved to Ted and Bebe (Winford's oldest child)—each representing their fathers' interests. The house desperately needed some capital expenditures, but no agreement could be reached about what to do or how, or whose money would pay for it! The fact that we were still living in the house rent-free was a stumbling block, since any improvement to the house was seen by Winford's children as a benefit to us. Sadly, it was difficult for them to think of the house as a separate entity worthy of preservation in and of itself whether we were there or not. But who else would care about it as much as we did? It wasn't really rentable due to water and sewage issues, and would renters take care of it? No one in the family was willing and able to take on the financial burden of buying and restoring it. It became clear that it would have to be sold, yet even that option proved difficult, since a potential buyer had to deal with a trust represented by two "sides" that weren't on the same page, and had to negotiate with each other through lawyers. Yes, it was a sad mess.

Enter Paul and Pat Hornback, who leased out the farming on Chenoweth Farm. They had already restored and added to an even older Thomas home (The Old Place), around the corner on Cropper Road, as their family home. Although it took lengthy negotiations,

Paul's proposal to buy the Big House along with 200 acres (which he could farm to help pay for restoring the house), finally met with everybody's approval. The concept of keeping the farm together *as a farm* had been drilled into the family by BAT II, so no one wanted to see it developed. Pat had *ideas* to turn the house into an event center.

After years of family disagreement, agonizing, and uncertainty, the closing for the sale of the house was accomplished in April of 2014. We all felt like throwing a party! But it was a little too early to celebrate. Another mountain had to be scaled, namely, *getting out of the house!* Lots of people move every day, right? Were you listening when I told you about all those records, memorabilia, and just stuff-that-could-not-be-thrown-away residing in the attic? When I told you how big the house was? When I mentioned all the rusted things hanging around the farm yards? And all that antique furniture and china and silver that nobody nowadays wants? And all the things that BA II and Vestina neglected to take with them when they died? (Like their underwear. Yes, it was still packed up in the attic!) The Hornbacks turned out to be a Godsend in more ways than one. They were actually *interested* in those old records, receipts, and furniture that represented a time gone by. We accepted their buyout offer, such that most of the contents of the house passed to them with the house. What a relief! We kept all our personal possessions, family items that had been requested by one descendant or another, and important family records. We said goodbye to everything else. May Paul and Pat be able to use it to create a place full of history to slow down and reflect upon.

We had from April until September of 2014 to remove our selves and belongings from the house. In the meantime, we were living in a house owned by someone else. Though there were some communication snafus to work through, both the owner and resident families weathered these five months, and we're still good neighbors.

What did we do for five months? First of all, we had a wedding at the house. Lydia (middle daughter) had planned her wedding in May, and had her heart set on having it at the house that she loved. The Hornbacks gave us every support to allow this to happen. To protect their investment, Pat decreed that the two ancient oaks close to the house had to come down. The Bur Oak in front had a vertical crack and was leaning toward the house. It had to be taken down in stages and most of it was gone by the summer, while the Chinquapin Oak on the West side was taken down later in the year. Both of them were only supported by about twelve inches of cambium and sapwood around the outside. All of the heartwood was gone and the space was hollow.

Bur (left) and Chinquapin (right). Notice Lydia and Serena at the Bur oak's base

Post tree removal. The house had never seen so much sun since it was first built!

Stump of the Chinquapin Oak. It was very sad to see two such majestic and ancient trees be cut down, but as you can see from the picture (the Bur oak was just as bad) there was not much left holding them up.

Lydia Bell Thomas Sherrer's wedding, May 24, 2014

During the spring and summer, Pat also worked to seal the outside envelope of the house and protect the leaded-glass windows. I dug up most of my perennials and moved them to Ted's parents' house. Pat pulled out most of the shrubs to facilitate work on the house. We sorted and packed and sweated through the summer, and finally mostly completed our move by September. We moved to the lower level of the BAT III house to help care for Ted's parents, both of whom had Alzheimer's. It was the end of an era for Chenoweth House, and the end of a twenty-six-year sojourn for us, but we were ready to move on.

Chenoweth House was ready to be reborn as Heritage House.

Part 3: The Third and Fourth Generations—1985 - 2014

Heritage House repainted and awaiting further restoration, 2015

APPENDIX: THE THOMAS GENERATIONS R.E. CHENOWETH FARM

Generation 1: **Morris** and Mary Thomas (arrived in PA from Wales 1768) 11 children:

Owen, Jeptha, Hannah, Elizabeth, Susan, Sarah, Rachel, John, Elisha, David, **Oswald**

Generation 2: **Oswald** (1769-1853), m. (1793) Mary Poage in Harrodsburg, KY 13 children:

Cassandra, Morris, Anna, Elizabeth (Betsy), Lindsey, Paulina, **Wilson J.**, John Ambrose, Harriet, Preston, Edwin, Martha, Mary Poage

Generation 3: **Wilson** (1806 – 1887), m. (1832) Nancy Gulick Johnston (1807-1901) 5 children:

Stephen, George, **Wilson John** (born John Lindsey, later John Wilson, then Wilson John), Sarah (Sallie), **Benjamin Allen** (BA I)

Generation 4a: **WJ** (1837-1925), m. (1879) Mary H. Thomas (1857-1918) no children

Generation 4b: **BA I** (1842-1912), m. (1887) Henrietta Stout (1863-1897) 1 child:
Ben Allen II

Generation 5: **BA II** (1890-1985), m. (1919) Vestina Bailey (1894-1984) 2 children:
Ben Allen III, Winford

Generation 6a: **BA III** (1920-2016), m. (1952) Emily A. Nichols (1928-2016) 4 children:
Edward (Ted), Lucy, Stephen, Daniel

Generation 6b: **Winford** (1924-2011), m. (1951) Betty E. Ball (1929-1970) 2 children:
Betty B., Ben Allen IV

Generation 7: **Ted** (1953-), m. (1981) Mary E. (Beth) Weringo (1955-) 4 children:
Sarah, Andrew (d. 2005), Lydia, Serena

Generation 8a: Sarah (1984-), m. (2008) Rainey C. Hartman (1980-) 5 children:
William, Edward, Sawyer, Miles, Ainsley

Generation 8b: Lydia (1989-), m. (2014) David Sherrer (1981-) 2 children:
Wesley, Elliot

ABOUT THE AUTHOR

Beth Thomas graduated from the College of William & Mary with a Bachelors in Psychology, and Virginia Commonwealth University with a Masters in Social Work. Her career has spanned many fields, from Social Work, Child Development, and Education, to Geriatrics and Bookkeeping. In all of these endeavors except the first, her focus has been on home and family: raising 4 children and educating them at home through high school, caring for 2 parents with Alzheimers, and helping in the family businesses. For this reason, this little volume about the home that nurtured her family for 26 years holds a special place in her heart.

Her previous writing career has included school and VBS curriculum, theater material for the local homeschool co-op, and annual family newsletters. She lives in Shelbyville, KY, with her husband and various lifeforms around the farm. When not managing the farm bookkeeping, she enjoys reading, gardening, scrapbooking, and spending time with her daughters and grandchildren.

www.ingramcontent.com/pod-product-compliance
Lightning Source LLC
Chambersburg PA
CBHW040203100526
44592CB00006B/88